APOSTOLIC METRONS

Written by: Chief Apostle Joseph L. Prude

GREAT PROGRESS
GREAT PROGRESS
GREAT PROGRESS
SAITH THE LORD

APOSTOLIC METRONS

Copyright © 2015 by Joseph L. Prude

Cover Designed by

Edited by: Apostle Barbara W. Erkins

Formatted by: Apostle Sandra Prude Formatted by: Apostle Noreen Battle

Scripture quotations are from:

The Holy Bible, King James Version, Holman Christian Standard Bible, and the American Standard Version

Visit the author's website at: www.AJP Ministries.com

ISBN 978-1-5136-1835-7

Printed in the United States of America

Acknowledgments

Finally...a book filled with the revelatory truths whose time has come. Apostle Prude has taken on the monumental task of simplifying the understanding of right apostolic order in a most exemplary approach. In his book, "Apostolic Metrons," he brings such a crisp, keen clarity to apostolic endorsement, apostolic anointing and measure of rule, just to touch on a few of the topics Apostle Prude addresses. This is a great work of importance for the entire Body of Christ. A must read for the ecclesia.

Apostle Barbara Erkins Key of Life Ministries

Apostolic Metrons must become part of the foundational arsenal of all those who seek or are scheduled for apostolic release. It gives great clarity and understanding to the measures, movements, and mass of apostolic assignments, protocols and proclivities. I wish I had had this book over 26 years ago when I was ordained as an apostle. It has helped to open my eyes to a greater dimension regarding the apostolic and its pliable nature, measures, and purposes that literally vary according to assignment, individuals, purpose, and grace. Every apostolic community needs this book to operate more effectively, according to a greater understanding. In all your getting....get Apostolic Metrons!

Dr. Clifford E. Turner
Chief Apostle
The Liberty International Network

Apostolic Metrons

As a chiropractor makes adjustments to the body, to correct things that are out of alignment, so does the masterfully written book Apostolic Metrons set out to adjust the Body of Christ's understanding of the apostolic realm and the Apostle's measure of rule. This book is a "must read" because it establishes why the Body of Christ and those who are called apostolically need to have a "clear and accurate understanding" of their measure of rule and the limits of their divine authority. For too long, people in their ignorance have surmised that Apostles have a universal call that gives them unlimited authority. The error in this thinking has brought much confusion, reproach and embarrassment in the Body of Christ.

Pastor Billy and Prophet Cynthia Thompson
Jesus People Proclaim International Church
Deerfield Beach, Florida

God is calling for divine order in this hour and Apostle Joseph Prude challenges the renegade and undisciplined to come into divine alignment to discover the 5 W's (who, what, when, where and why) of their apostolic call. Once a basic understanding is established people will not only know what an Apostle is but they will understand that there is diversity in the Apostle's mantle and a multidimensional function in each individual's call. As God restores the office of the Apostle, this book will undoubtedly serve as a apostolic guidepost to help leaders and laypersons alike gain knowledge and draw insight into the varied dimensions apostolic metrons.

Foreword

I began sensing my apostolic call back in late 2008. Shortly thereafter, I began receiving all kinds of prophecies from varying mature leaders concerning the call. I had absolutely no idea what this meant – outside of what I managed to glean from the scriptures myself. I bought books, sat in on a few conference calls, read articles and saw absolutely no reflection of myself. The only thing I knew for sure during that season was that God called me to be His Master Scribe. He placed an unquenchable passion in my heart to build a scribal nation globally, to restore the ministry of the scribe back to His congregation; to ignite scribes with a passion to preserve and protect His word and the work of Holy Spirit in the earth; and to duplicate this calling and mandate in others. This was a far cry from an apostolic work I saw in my limited environment.

It was not until Apostle Joseph Prude was led by Holy Spirit to reach out to me some four years later that my life and purpose began to take shape. He was the first person in the history of my walk with the Lord to completely "get" who God had called me to be in the Kingdom. I was experiencing extreme frustration and disillusionment within the church as a whole; and was troubled deeply concerning my calling to ministry. Though I never mentioned it, I actually thought I had missed God. There was absolutely no model from the 20th century church that fit who I was and who I was becoming.

One afternoon meeting with Apostle Prude changed all this for me. I was called to life through the extremely accurate prophetic ministry resting upon his life. I was affirmed in my pioneering purpose in scribal ministry; and given clear instructions concerning what it meant to embrace my apostolic metron.

Listen, the only thing I heard about apostles were that they raised up sons, traveled and planted churches. I was sure, however, that the structure of the 19th and 20th century church was shifting rapidly. Yet, no one in my direct sphere of influence was talking about apostolic reformation or the raising up of specialists who would master their metrons and operate in fresh, new areas of apostolic authority.

Apostle Prude's decades of wisdom, authority in the apostolic and keen discernment was foundational in renewing my strength, rooting me in my own identity and launching me fully into my apostolic mantle.

His latest book, *Apostolic Metrons*, takes what I have learned up to this point to an entirely new spiritual level. I have never, ever heard anything like the revelatory message between these pages before. Not only has razor-blade alignment come to me as a result of the intense and detailed teachings inside this book regarding understanding your measure, but I have a greater appreciation for what God has placed in my hands.

Apostle Prude uses the ministry of the Apostle Paul to provide a blueprint of what it looks like to operate in one's "apostolic metron" while at the same time weeding out true apostles from the false, and eradicating an extensive amount of error in the midst of Christ's body.

I must warn you: Get ready to repent. Get ready for Holy Spirit to realign you in your thinking, and maybe even in your perception of the call on your life.

Do not mistake *Apostolic Metrons* for just another book on the apostolic. It is a call to truth, to destiny, to purpose… and into a renewed fear of the Lord.

There is absolutely too much at stake in this dispensation of the gospel to ignore the breath of God between these pages.

Thank you Apostle Prude for helping me embrace, love, realign and navigate within my apostolic measure of rule. The best is yet to come.

Apostle Theresa Harvard Johnson

Table of Contents

CHAPTER 1

WHAT IS AN APOSTOLIC METRON

The virus of misunderstanding and ignorance cannot hinder this current apostolic restoration. Those of us who are more familiar with apostolic functionality have finally gained insight and now understand that there are apostles of many different classes and dispensations. Some dispensations of this apostolic restoration have levels and sub levels. These many different levels need to be clearly understood. There are also apostolic seasons and times, various branches and various streams and rivers of the apostolic; with their tributaries. These areas are critical and must be understood. In this book we will attempt to do all we can by the leading of the Holy Spirit to give accuracy and clarity in these areas. Apostles have a mandate to bring revelatory truths to the forefront and to teach in such a way as to bring correction to places of error and misunderstanding.

What exactly is a Metron?

The word metron is actually a derivative of the word metronome. It, in fact, means a measured and specific part or portion. In some cases it can even relate to borders and coastlines. The Greek word metronome is also a term that is used for musical measurements. The metronome is a device that measures beats and timing. To be able to fully understand and function properly in this current apostolic restoration it is absolutely critical to understand apostolic metrons, as well as the metrons of the various apostolic classes of apostles. Without clear and accurate understanding of apostolic metrons, we walk in places of trespass and violation of kingdom laws; this results in our bringing reproach and dishonor to the kingdom of God.

Metron defined:

1. A place were one has apostolic grace to operate.

2. A place were one has divine authority.

3. A place where grace confirms one's measure.

4. A place of specific assignment

5. A place of apostolic territorial dominion

CHAPTER 2

UNDERSTANDING APOSTOLIC
MEASURE OF RULE

2 Corinthians 10:12-16 (KJV)

12. For we dare not make ourselves of the number, or compare ourselves with some that commend themselves: but they measuring themselves by themselves, and comparing themselves among themselves, are not wise.

13. But we will not boast of things without our measure, but according to the measure of the rule which God hath distributed to us, a measure to reach even unto you.

14. For we stretch not ourselves beyond our measure, as though we reached not unto you: for we are come as far as to you also in preaching the gospel of Christ:

15. Not boasting of things without our measure, that is, of other men's labours; but having hope, when your faith is increased, that we shall be enlarged by you according to our rule abundantly,

16. To preach the gospel in the regions beyond you, and not to boast in another man's line of things made ready to our hand.

It is critical to understand the concept of "measure of rule," if you will effectively operate in kingdom government. Every man, every office, every call has an assigned measure. As we have already stated, the Greek word for measure is the word (metronome). This word means a measured pace, a measured step, a specific portion or place. This word is typically associated with musical terminology and is used in syncopation of beats or measurement of music.

Paul made reference to men who measured incorrectly; they measured among themselves by themselves. Their measure was not in accordance with a divine standard but in accordance with a human standard. Also in verse thirteen, Paul references the need to stay within his measure. Even though Paul was a chief apostle, he still understood that he had a measure of rule. There are many today who think that they have a universal, unlimited, apostolic call, but in reality that is not so. Even the greatest apostles have limited measure. If you will notice, in verse thirteen Paul speaks of the distribution of his measure. In other words, he speaks of the delegated amount of authority that has been given to him by the Lord Jesus. How often have we seen people who supposedly are apostles, yet with no concept or idea of measure of rule? This has brought much reproach and embarrassment to the body of Christ. There are men who have actually walked into churches in an attempt to operate out of their claim to be apostles in a function of greater latitude than they have been given. Because they did not understand that their measure of rule only pertained to their designated place of assignment, these unfortunate encounters met with grave consequences.

There is a Kingdom law called "the law of divine measure". If more believers understood this spiritual law, the church would be in better shape today. This law is first mentioned in the book of Leviticus.

Leviticus 35-36, *"Ye shall do no unrighteousness in judgment, in meteyard, in weight, or in measure. Just balances, just weights, a just ephah, and a just hin, shall ye have: I am the LORD your God, which brought you out of the land of Egypt."*

Scripture clearly implies that if you go beyond your measure you are operating in a place of unrighteousness. God is very serious about our need to understand our measure of rule and the limits of divine authority. If we refuse to take this under consideration, then herein lies the reason for so much confusion today in this current apostolic restoration. We have people who claim to have an apostolic call, but cannot tell you the measure of their call. Paul was always very specific as he would point out his measure of rule. Paul understood he was an apostle to the Gentiles. That was his measure, that was his jurisdiction, it was his metron.

Romans 11:13 (KJV)

13. For I speak to you Gentiles, inasmuch as I am the apostle of the Gentiles, I magnify mine office:

Paul was very plain spoken in his description of his specific call to the Gentiles. He could tell you with absolute certainty the measure he was given, when he was sent and where he was sent. If you notice he said, "...I magnify mine office." In other words, Paul says, I continue to work on the need to master the measure I have been given. If you say you are called to be an apostle and the Lord Jesus has called you, then it is imperative for you to understand that you were never called as a universal apostle, who has been delegated universal apostolic authority and able to run "willy - nilly" any and everywhere with absolutely no specific assignment. What is required of you, however, is to master the measure that you have been given by God.

Acts 9:4-6 (KJV)

4. And he fell to the earth, and heard a voice saying unto him, Saul, Saul, why persecutest thou me?

5. And he said, Who art thou, Lord? And the Lord said, I am Jesus whom thou persecutest: it is hard for thee to kick against the pricks.

6. And he trembling and astonished said, Lord, what wilt thou have me to do? And the Lord said unto him, Arise, and go into the city, and it shall be told thee what thou must do.

When the Lord Jesus appeared to Paul, he told him "arise and go into the city and it shall be told you what you must do." Paul did not receive a general apostolic call to be an apostle anywhere and everywhere, but what Paul was given, however, was a specific charge to the Gentiles. Paul had delegated to him his metron, a specific measure of assignment; it was also referred to as his jurisdiction. In Scripture we can see that whenever there is any violation of measure, God takes it very, very seriously. This brings us to another Kingdom law, it is the law of trespass.

Leviticus 5:4-6 (ASV)

4. Or if any one swear rashly with his lips to do evil, or to do good, whatsoever it be that a man shall utter rashly with an oath, and it be hid from him; when he knoweth of it, then he shall be guilty in one of these things.

5. And it shall be, when he shall be guilty in one of these things, that he shall confess that wherein he hath sinned:

6. and he shall bring his trespass-offering unto Jehovah for his sin which he hath sinned, a female from the flock, a lamb or a goat, for a sin-offering; and the priest shall make atonement for him as concerning his sin.

We see in these verses the sin of trespass was described in broad terminology. There are many ways one could walk in trespass. One could walk in trespass by words, by deeds, and even in an attempt to do the right thing. The truth we extrapolate out of this, however, is that if you make a confession that God has called you and designated you as an apostle, but through presumption you begin to act illegally and without a slated jurisdiction or license, you have, by default, stepped into the area of trespass. I know this may seem unfair and harsh, but it is reality. If you break the law of trespass, albeit your intentions are good or you were not even aware that you trespassed...you are still guilty of trespass. How sad it is today that we have so many who think that this new apostolic restoration is just another passing fad that they can presumptuously walk into without consequences.

PROPHETIC WORD

The word of the Lord comes and says: This is the day and this is the hour that I come to correct things that are out of line. My people, it has grieved me much, as divine law has been violated over and over by the sin of presumption. Many have walked in areas to which I have never called you. You have brought great confusion to My body. It caused My people to wonder whether or not My word and My principles were really true. This is the hour I send forth a corrective word to repair the damage that has been done in My body. There are many of you, the Lord says as you read this, that are beginning to identify your personal misalignment. If you would take heed to this and let Me repair you and put you in proper alignment, then I the Lord shall forgive you, correct you and set you on a course that will help My body. I come to visit My body and remove from it all that I did not place in it. Every tree I did not plant shall be plucked up in this season. This is the hour that I, the Lord, bring correction.

Saith the Lord

1 Corinthians 9:1-2 (KJV)

1. Am I not an apostle? Am I not free? Have I not seen Jesus Christ our Lord? are not ye my work in the Lord?

2. If I be not an apostle unto others, yet doubtless I am to you: for the seal of mine apostleship are ye in the Lord.

As a called apostle, there must be a divinely assigned metron or jurisdiction. Paul himself said in this particular passage of scripture that there existed a group of people Paul recognized to whom he was not called. As great an apostle as Paul was, he still understood his measure of rule was not assigned with this people group; Paul was not given to presumption in this regard.

This current violation of misunderstood jurisdiction is at epidemic proportions. Today amongst the body of Christ, there are renegade, so-called apostolic people who claim to have unlimited, unfettered and unrestrained apostolic authority. This disproportionate amount of damage to the body of Christ is through the misconception of one's measure of rule and assigned metrons. It is of key significance to understand that if God calls you to function in an apostolic office, then rest assured God will give you an apostolic assignment along with a very specific measure of rule and the clarity to know, apostolically, to whom you are called.

CHAPTER 3

VARIOUS KINDS OF APOSTOLIC METRONS AND DIMENSIONS

We are living in a very unique season. It is a season in which the Holy Spirit is beginning to restore the apostolic office. In the midst of today's restoration, however, it garners many questions as to the dimensions of an apostle's place of assignment, along with the fact that there seems to be so few verifiable checks and balances in place. Many people have a somewhat basic level of understanding as to what/who an apostle is. An apostle is One That Is Sent. In a more in depth and careful study of the word, 'sent /send' a greater insight and clarity is realized, which speaks to the various types of apostolic classes to be considered.

1 Corinthians 12:4-6 (KJV)

4. Now there are diversities of gifts, but the same Spirit.

5. And there are differences of administrations, but the same Lord.

6. And there are diversities of operations, but it is the same God which worketh all in all.

The Scripture plainly states that there are different kinds of operations. The Greek word for operations could also be translated as **flow**. In other words there are various ways, if you will, there are diverse and different ways that the apostolic office operates. There are various ways, diverse and different ways in which the apostolic office is administrated.

As we are in this time of divine restoration, we continue to get the much needed clarity and revelation as to what the apostolic office really is. As you look at different apostles in the manifestation of their calls, you will notice that no two apostles operate exactly the same. It is no different than a person reaching into a toolbox and taking out the appropriate tool for a specific task. There are various apostolic anointings to meet different needs and to perform different tasks. It is important to remember that it is the Holy Spirit that is operating in each one. The apostolic office is not expressed in one monolithic operation. There are many diverse manifestations of the apostolic office in the body of Christ. It is very important that we properly understand this so that we can work with God and not against Him.

CHAPTER 4

TEMPORARY APOSTLE

There is an apostolic class called the temporary apostle, which means one sent with a temporary apostolic anointing to complete a specific apostolic assignment. This particular apostolic expression has not been fully understood in the body of Christ. There are those who have been apostalized but not with a permanent apostolic anointing. They are sent for a specific task and given apostolic grace to perform that task. We can see this example in one sent out to pastor and plant a church. According to kingdom rules a church planter would need to be licensed in the spirit to have authority to birth a church. Planting a church is a spiritual performance and not a mere natural task. The authority to plant a church is purely apostolic. It is not something given at the behest of the missionary board or by a committee. It requires an apostolic anointing. If there is no apostolic anointing present, then the spirit realm would not respond to the effort to plant a church. Territorial and ruling satanic powers would not be moved. This is where the temporary apostolic anointing comes in to play. The Greek word for this anointing is the word pempo.

John 12:44-49 (KJV)

44. Jesus cried and said, He that believeth on me, believeth not on me, but on him that sent me.

45. And he that seeth me seeth him that sent me.

46. I am come a light into the world, that whosoever believeth on me should not abide in darkness.

47. And if any man hear my words, and believe not, I judge him not: for I came not to judge the world, but to save the world.

48. He that rejecteth me, and receiveth not my words, hath one that judgeth him: the word that I have spoken, the same shall judge him in the last day.

49. For I have not spoken of myself; but the Father which sent me, he gave me a commandment, what I should say, and what I should speak.

The word "sent" here in verse forty-nine is not the Greek word apostelos, which is the word commonly used for a sent one or apostle. It is the Greek word pempo. This word is different than the word apostelos, in that this is a temporary commission for a temporary assignment and not a permanent apostolic license.

Strong's Talking Greek & Hebrew Dictionary

Greek Word: πέμπω

Transliteration: pempō

Vine's Words: Send

Apparently a primary verb; to dispatch (from the subject view or point of departure, whereas hiemi [as a stronger form of eimi] refers rather to the object point or terminus ad quem, and <G4724>(stello) denotes properly the orderly motion involved) especially on a temporary errand; also to transmit, bestow, or wield: - send, thrust in.

Jesus used this word pempo to speak of His earthly ministry. Jesus was in fact saying that His apostolic mission to the earth was a temporary assignment; it was not a permanent apostolic assignment. So, Jesus did not use the word apostolic in speaking of His apostolic mission in this place. Jesus used the word pempo to speak of the temporary nature of His earthly assignment. It is important to understand that the Bible is a precision book and in this book, Jesus spoke in specifics as He communicated about Himself, His life and His mission.

Many times in the function of the fivefold ministry there is a need for apostolic performance in a given situation. God will release a pempo apostolic anointing upon a person or even a group of persons to perform a temporary apostolic task. We could call this a temporary apostolic license. Jesus used the term license when he made this statement in the gospel of John, "I go to prepare a place for you." The word "place" here, in the Greek, actually means a condition or license. Apostles, in fact, have a divine license to perform within a certain sphere of authority. We see and understand this more clearly when we go back and see the Old Testament term for apostle which is the word shelah. The Old Testament shelah was sent from the court of the Torah. They were given what were called letters granting them authority to act in behalf of the court of the Torah that sent them. This is what Paul meant when he spoke of being sent to both kill and lock up the brethren. He said he had letters or a license to act apostolically or as a Shelah, authorized by the court of the Torah.

In the natural, most licenses have a termination point. So it is with the temporary apostolic license; there is a point when the license expires. Tragically speaking, this has not been clearly understood nor communicated. The end result is that there are many who have received a temporary apostolic assignment to birth a church or perform an assignment, yet, when the license had actually expired spiritually; they unfortunately continued to call themselves Apostles, not understanding that the license had been terminated and that it had been terminated by God. This is why we see the body of Christ flooded with those that call themselves Apostles, but they have no divine evidence. We can readily find numerous examples of temporary assignments in Scripture. One of the clearest examples is when Abraham sent Eleazar out on assignment to find a wife for Isaac. Eleazar had a temporary apostolic license to go and obtain a wife for Isaac. The word shelah is used in reference to his commission to scout out this wife for Isaac. Eleazar, strictly in this instance, became an Old Testament pempo apostle.

Genesis 24:1-9 (KJV)

1. And Abraham was old, and well stricken in age: and the LORD had blessed Abraham in all things.

2. And Abraham said unto his eldest servant of his house, that ruled over all that he had, Put, I pray thee, thy hand under my thigh:

3. And I will make thee swear by the LORD, the God of heaven, and the God of the earth, that thou shalt not take a wife unto my son of the daughters of the Canaanites, among whom I dwell:

4. But thou shalt go unto my country, and to my kindred, and take a wife unto my son Isaac.

5. And the servant said unto him, Peradventure the woman will not be willing to follow me unto this land: must I needs bring thy son again unto the land from whence thou camest?

6. And Abraham said unto him, Beware thou that thou bring not my son thither again.

7. The LORD God of heaven, which took me from my father's house, and from the land of my kindred, and which spake unto me, and that sware unto me, saying, Unto thy seed will I give this land; he shall send his angel before thee, and thou shalt take a wife unto my son from thence.

8. And if the woman will not be willing to follow thee, then thou shalt be clear from this my oath: only bring not my son thither again.

9. And the servant put his hand under the thigh of Abraham his master, and sware to him

Abraham sent his servant out with a temporary apostolic mantle to obtain a wife for Isaac. When this temporary assignment was over, so was Eleazar's license. It is of the utmost importance for us to understand this process and how it relates to the temporary apostolic anointing; the pempo anointing. A lack of clarity in this area has brought much unnecessary confusion to the body of Christ. Please indulge me in my continued emphasis on the confusion to the body of Christ and our need to understand what we have done and what we are doing...this is serious. We see men and women going forward claiming to be apostles when, in fact, they have only had, for some season, a temporary apostolic anointing to perform a certain task. They have erroneously continued to use the title with no understanding that their license has expired.

John 16:5 (KJV)

5. But now I go my way to him that sent me; and none of you asketh me, Whither goest thou?

Again we see Jesus in this particular verse using the term pempo, to speak of the temporary nature of his apostolic mission. He was preparing to leave the Earth and informing the disciples that his ministry on the Earth in human form was temporary.

We see in scripture the temporary apostolic mantle that rests on John the Baptist. John himself spoke of the temporary nature of his being sent. John was one that clearly understood that he was temporarily assigned with an apostolic grace to go before the Messiah. He was in no way conflicted about his assignment, nor did he attempt to extend his license beyond measure.

John 1:33 (KJV)

33. And I knew him not: but he that sent me to baptize with water, the same said unto me, Upon whom thou shalt see the Spirit descending, and remaining on him, the same is he which baptizeth with the Holy Ghost.

Again, we see in this particular verse, the word sent; the Greek word pempo. Let us take a moment to reiterate, pempo means one sent on a temporary apostolic assignment. John clearly understood both the measure of his rule and his season. He had a pempo apostolic assignment as a forerunner to make preparation for the coming of the Messiah.

CHAPTER 5

THE ACCOMPANYING APOSTLE

Acts 20:4 (HCSB)

4. He was accompanied by Sopater son of Pyrrhus from Berea, Aristarchus and Secundus from Thessalonica, Gaius from Derbe, Timothy, and Tychicus and Trophimus from Asia.

There is another aspect of the apostolic metron, which we will call the accompanying apostle. This is a person or group of persons that has an apostolic license, but the license is only valid as long as they remain with the chief apostle that ordained them to be part of an apostolic company. This is, again, another area where there is tremendous lack of understanding. Many have been ordained apostles as part of an apostolic team with a specific apostolic assignment within the confines of that team. They function well, apostolically, as long as they remain connected with the chief apostle that brought them in as members of the said apostolic team. We clearly see an example of this in the life and ministry of Paul. Paul had a very large and diverse apostolic team. It was a team made up of both male and female apostles who accompanied him in ministry at different seasons. This class of apostles are referred to as accompanying apostles. We can take a look at this in the Greek:

2 Corinthians 12:18 (KJV)

18. I desired Titus, and with him I sent a brother. Did Titus make a gain of you? walked we not in the same spirit? walked we not in the same steps?

The Greek word for sent, as it applies here, is synapostellos. The word means to be sent alongside another. In this case it means that the apostolic anointing operates synergistically. This is not an apostolic license that is legal and valid apart from relationship with the sender. If you notice, Paul said, "...walked we not in the same spirit... walked we not in the same steps.?" In other words, to maintain this class of apostolic anointing, you must walk in step, remain in step and in the same spirit with the one that sent you and apostalized you for this particular task.

.Strong's Talking Greek & Hebrew Dictionary

Greek Strong's Number: 4882

Green Word: συναποστέλλω

Transliteration: synapostellō

from <G4862> (sun) and <G649> (apostello); to despatch (on an errand) in company with :- send with.

We can see the use of this term again in the Greek translation of the Old Testament called the Septuagint.

Exodus 33:2

2. And I will send at the same time my angel before thy face, and he shall cast out the Amorite and the Chettite, and the Pherezite and Gergesite, and Evite, and Jebusite, and Chananite.

This particular verse is taken directly from the English translation of the Greek Septuagint. The word here is the Greek word synapostellos. Again, this word means to send with or to come alongside another; this simply means that this particular class of apostle is one that is valid as long as they remain connected to the one that sent them. They do not have an independent and separate apostolic license, at least not as of yet.

This place is normally a temporary place of apostolic preparatory training for anyone who is being prepared for a full apostolic license. For the sake of clarity, we will call this an apostolic apprenticeship. This apprenticeship is like what we see in the natural with workmen in the trades. Anyone in the trades is more than likely in a union. The union has mandatory, non-negotiable requirements to become licensed in the trades. ..it is not selective or elective; you go through all the required levels or you are out! The unions refer to this time of training and refining as the necessary season of apprenticeship. In the natural, one cannot become fully licensed as a plumber, a pipe fitter or carpenter without completing the season of apprenticeship. Unfortunately, so often in the kingdom, because of pride, there are one's who are unwilling to walk through this temporary season of being an accompanying apostle. They want to step right into a full apostolic office, which for these persons it becomes an un-validated place, even at this entry level. The heavens will not even recognize or witness to their apostolic declaration, not at this juncture. It is very important to remember that the apostolic office is a heavenly office. If it is not validated in the heavens, it has no effectiveness in the earth. Furthermore, Paul was very plain spoken with regard to this issue in the book of Ephesians, in his description of how apostles should operate.

Ephesians 6:12 (KJV)

12. For we wrestle not against flesh and blood, but against principalities, against powers, against the rulers of the darkness of this world, against spiritual wickedness in high places.

If there is no legitimate apostolic license, there is no ability to wrestle against principalities, powers and the rulers of the darkness of this world. The powers of wickedness, just like heaven, will recognize whether or not you have done due diligence...don't fool yourself!

This particular verse is taken directly from the English translation of the Greek Septuagint. The word here is the Greek word synapostellos. Again, this word means to send with or to come alongside another; this simply means that this particular class of apostle is one that is valid as long as they remain connected to the one that sent them. They do not have an independent and separate apostolic license, at least not as of yet.

This place is normally a temporary place of apostolic preparatory training for anyone who is being prepared for a full apostolic license. For the sake of clarity, we will call this an apostolic apprenticeship. This apprenticeship is like what we see in the natural with workmen in the trades. Anyone in the trades is more than likely in a union. The union has mandatory, non-negotiable requirements to become licensed in the trades. ...it is not selective or elective; you go through all the required levels or you are out! The unions refer to this time of training and refining as the necessary season of apprenticeship. In the natural, one cannot become fully licensed as a plumber, a pipe fitter or carpenter without completing the season of apprenticeship. Unfortunately, so often in the kingdom, because of pride, there are one's who are unwilling to walk through this temporary season of being an accompanying apostle. They want to step right into a full apostolic office, which for these persons it becomes an un-validated place, even at this entry level. The heavens will not even recognize or witness to their apostolic declaration, not at this juncture. It is very important to remember that the apostolic office is a heavenly office. If it is not validated in the heavens, it has no effectiveness in the earth. Furthermore, Paul was very plain spoken with regard to this issue in the book of Ephesians, in his description of how apostles should operate.

Ephesians 6:12 (KJV)

12. For we wrestle not against flesh and blood, but against principalities, against powers, against the rulers of the darkness of this world, against spiritual wickedness in high places.

If there is no legitimate apostolic license, there is no ability to wrestle against principalities, powers and the rulers of the darkness of this world. The powers of wickedness, just like heaven, will recognize whether or not you have done due diligence...don't fool yourself!

CHAPTER 6

PAUL'S APOSTOLIC TEAM

Romans 16:21-23 (HCSB)

21. Timothy, my coworker, and Lucius, Jason, and Sosipater, my fellow countrymen, greet you.

22. I Tertius, who wrote this letter, greet you in the Lord.

23. Gaius, who is host to me and to the whole church, greets you. Erastus, the city treasurer, and our brother Quartus greet you

In this verse we see Paul's apostolic team. If you notice, Paul uses a term in verse twenty-one, co-worker or co-laborer. In the King James Version it is translated workfellow, which again speaks of the apostolic position, that these accompanying apostles were in. They were:

- Timothy

- Lucius

- Jason

- Sosipater

- Tertius

The word workfellow here, has the same prefix as the word synapostilos The prefix is again the Greek word synergy:

Greek Word: συνεργός

Transliteration: synergos

Vine's Words: Companion, Helper, Fellow-helper, Worker, Workfellow, Fellow Workers, Workman

Usage Notes:

English Words used in KJV:

fellow labourer 4

helper 3

fellow helper 2

fellow workers 1

work fellow 1

labourer together with 1

companion in labour 1

[Total Count: 13]

From a presumed compound of <G4862> (sun) and the base of <G2041> (ergon); a co-laborer, i.e. coadjutor :- companion in labour, (fellow-) helper (-labourer, -worker), labourer together with, workfellow.

As we read these verses, we see that these apostles were accompanying apostles who worked in conjunction with Paul. They were men that understood that the measure of their apostolic ministry was connected to their relationship with Paul. Let me say that again. They were men that understood that the measure of their apostolic ministry was connected to their relationship with Paul. These men were, in fact, in apostolic apprenticeship, which again, as we mentioned previously, is a temporary position; an intermediary step, if you will, before there is a full apostolic license.

Sadly enough, there are an innumerable amount of folks today who are too proud and too arrogant to walk in this temporary position. They want to skip steps, not pay the price, not pay their dues, yet, they most assuredly want to receive the honor. One of the best reasons I can give you as to why apostles should take this temporary step is because it allows them time to fully understand the measure of the apostolic call. If you look carefully at Paul's apostolic team, you will see that each one of the apostles in his team had a different level of mastery and had skill sets for different tasks. There are no two apostles who are exactly the same in function and operation.

It is of the utmost importance to note here the ongoing principal of seedtime and harvest. If you expect to function with a full apostolic license, then God in His great wisdom, is allowing you an opportunity to sow a seed of labor, effort and faithfulness into another person's apostolic work. As a result of this time of seeding, you have created your own future by faithfully seeding your gifts, talent and your time into another man's field.

CHAPTER 7

APOSTOLIC TRANSFER

Luke 23:6-7 (KJV)

6. When Pilate heard of Galilee, he asked whether the man were a Galilaean.

7. And as soon as he knew that he belonged unto Herod's jurisdiction, he sent him to Herod, who himself also was at Jerusalem at that time.

There are times when there is a need for apostolic transfer. This is very difficult for most apostolic people; because it requires a process of death to self and one's own personal ambition. In the verses we have just read, we are aware that what has transpired is an apostolic transfer, authorized based on jurisdiction.

In these particular verses we are able to extrapolate an understandable truth from the Word, even though we are aware that this entire encounter between Jesus and Herod was fueled entirely by a politically negative, motivational impetus. Pilate attempts to rid himself of the responsibility for Jesus but he did not want the burden of having to make an unrighteous decision. Once Pilate understood that Jesus fell under the jurisdiction of Herod he was quick to send him to Herod. The Greek term for sent here is the word anapempō, this usage means to send up to a higher authority.

There will be numerous occasions within the operation of apostolic ministry where a need will arise for divine apostolic transfer. It appears that we do not readily see this function as operational within the body of Christ today; nevertheless, it is still a divine apostolic principle.

Let us take for instance that we have a student who graduates from the junior high school level to go on to the senior high school level. The teachers and principals who comprise the administrative staff of the junior high school are not in any way offended because it is now time for this student's promotion. The administrative staff has operated with the student in order to ensure his academic accomplishments, which came about by way of the staff's administrative measure of rule and authority.

The administrative staff has been both duly recognized and compensated, not to mention, even awarded for operating at the level in which they were to function. In the administration's mind there is no sense of personal failure or loss as it pertains to the move of the student to the next level. In fact, the staff recognizes and celebrates with the student his completion of the required fields of study which now results in his graduation to the next level.

The teachers in a junior high school recognize the fact that they have both trained and equipped the students to go on to senior high school.

This is the order of things in the natural and it should also be the same as it relates to that which is spiritual.

All apostles, legitimately called of God, have what is known as an apostolic grace. Please note, the apostolic grace on them does not necessarily apply to everyone. There will be those that belong to your tribe who will ultimately become sons and daughters, as well as those who do not belong to your tribe even though you may help them for a season. This is the area where you need to be sensitive to the Will of God as it pertains to apostolic transfer.

We will take another look at this concept in scripture as we browse through the letter written to Philemon by Paul.

Philemon 1:1-2 (KJV)

1. Paul, a prisoner of Jesus Christ, and Timothy our brother, unto Philemon our dearly beloved, and fellowlaborer

2. And to our beloved Apphia, and Archippus our fellowsoldier, and to the church in thy house:

Paul is imprisoned in Rome and writes to a dear brother by the name of Philemon. It is important to recognize and carefully examine how Paul addresses Philemon. You will notice Paul refers to Philemon as a fellow laborer. This term was readily used at that time in history by active apostles as they made reference to others who were apostles as well. We see this term used repeatedly in scripture as apostles addressed one another.

Romans 16:21 (KJV)

21. Timotheus my workfellow, and Lucius, and Jason, and Sosipater, my kinsmen, salute you.

In each of these verses we see the same Greek word used to describe the relationship between these apostles. The Greek word used is the word synergos. This word was often used by apostles to denote other apostles who were of the same class apostolically. This term was used with regard to Philemon. So, from this we deduce that Paul was writing a letter to a fellow apostle concerning the young man. Now we want to be very clear here;

Paul was the person of significance, Paul was the central character in this entire dynamic, strictly because Paul is the point person the Lord uses to bring this young man to a place of conversion. The caveat, however, is that Paul still recognized this newly converted young man was not his spiritual son.

Please catch the significance in what Paul understood. Paul knew it was imperative for him to hand this young man off to whom he was assigned. So Paul sent him up to Philemon by way of an apostolic transfer so that Philemon would ultimately have divine authority over him. Here again, Paul, even as a chief apostle, understands clearly his measure of rule or his metron. By the same token if we, in the body of Christ, understood this dynamic more precisely, it would serve to relieve us of much conflict. There is a specific time of apostolic transfer that requires apostolic integrity and character. Paul had such a handle on this concept, that the distinction between himself, Apollos and Cephas was easily denoted in his writings.

1. Corinthians 3:5-8 (KJV)

5. Who then is Paul, and who is Apollos, but ministers by whom ye believed, even as the Lord gave to every man?

6. I have planted, Apollos watered; but God gave the increase.

7. So then neither is he that planteth any thing, neither he that watereth; but God that giveth the increase.

8. Now he that planteth and he that watereth are one: and every man shall receive his own reward according to his own labour.

I love how Paul pays no laud to himself about who he is and over who he thinks he should have power or control. Paul, in a very matter-of-fact modality, states that he planted, Apollo watered, but God gave the increase. There will be times as an apostle, when you will plant the seed in a person's life and you may think that they will continue on with you as an apostolic son or daughter, but it is not God's plan. God will have you perform an apostolic transfer if you will allow Him. These sons/daughters may ultimately be watered by someone else, but God will give the increase and every man shall receive his own reward according to his labor. As apostles, we must realize that we can't hold on to everyone. Apostolic definition defines that part of what we are called to do is to release people and send them forth. Remember, your reward comes not just by your children, but through your children's children.

Proverbs 17:6 (KJV)

6. Children's children are the crown of old men; and the glory of children are their fathers.

When the Holy Spirit is able to fully restore this particular truth, we will see the kingdom operate more efficiently instead of us fighting and warring over what we think are spoils. Due to the lack of understanding in this area, there is great contention among apostles. There is not one New Testament example I can point to, in which we see apostles warring over the ownership of people. Thank God that we have different classes of apostles; this is what helps the fruitfulness, the productivity and diversity of the body of Christ.

PROPHETIC WORD

The word of the Lord comes and says: I am the Lord God who rules over everything. I am Jesus, the one that died upon the cross, and set you forth as my apostles to be under shepherds. You are to build my servants and construct my servants. I did not call you to be as Pharaohs, to dominate them or to rule over them; but to nurture and develop them. If you would do this safely, I, even the Lord; shall give you a great reward in that day when you stand before Me.

CHAPTER 8

APOSTOLIC RELEASE

Acts 13:3-4 (KJV)

3. And when they had fasted and prayed, and laid their hands on them, they sent them away.

4. So they, being sent forth by the Holy Ghost, departed unto Seleucia; and from thence they sailed to Cyprus.

In this particular set of verses, we see where Paul and Barnabas were sent forth into apostolic ministry. Apostolic release is critical in this current apostolic restoration.Every apostolic father's resume should include within the contents of that resume, those sons / daughters that have been both sent and released by him. Regrettably, there are apostolic fathers who have "lead their sons and daughters on"and these 'offspring' were in hopes that they would be sent, when in fact, these apostolic fathers never had intentions of releasing them at all. This is dishonest and leads to a disintegration in trust in the apostolic ministry. The Greek word for the word sent is the word:

Strong's Talking Greek & Hebrew Dictionary.

Greek Strong's Number: 630

Greek Word: ἀπολύω

Transliteration: apolyō

The word means the following, to release, to depart, to divorce, at liberty, to send forth.

Every apostolic father should be able to show forth, based on his or her spiritual legacy, the fact that they have sent out and released apostolic sons and daughters. If an apostolic father does not have this as part of his or her legacy, then the validity of that apostolic mantle would certainly have to come into question. Scripture plainly tells us that children's children are the crowns of old men.

Proverbs 17:6 (KJV)

6. Children's children are the crown of old men; and the glory of children are their fathers.

The apostle finds his vindication and his validation in the fact that his sons and daughters are able to go forward. These sons and daughters carry the fragrance of the house in which they were birthed and raised as they go forth, and they, too, produce children that carry the same spirit; the spirit of the house of the chief father.

Correspondingly, apostolic sons and daughters who have been under the tutelage and training of an apostolic father should be willing to wait for the day of their Apolyo. There are many apostles today that have no traceable and verifiable lineage. It is very important for one to receive a divine endorsement by an apostolic father. There are many that have never had their own personal apolyo. Even Jesus, experientially had a day of 'Apolyo endorsement,' so to speak, when His Father spoke and said, "...this is my beloved Son in whom I am well pleased." We see another clear example of the need for the validation of lineage in the story of Saul and Samuel.

1 Samuel 10:9-12 (KJV)

9. And it was so, that when he had turned his back to go from Samuel, God gave him another heart: and all those signs came to pass that day.

10. And when they came thither to the hill, behold, a company of prophets met him; and the Spirit of God came upon him, and he prophesied among them.

11. And it came to pass, when all that knew him beforetime saw that, behold, he prophesied among the prophets, then the people said one to another, What is this that is come unto the son of Kish? Is Saul also among the prophets?

12. And one of the same place answered and said, But who is their father? Therefore it became a proverb, Is Saul also among the prophets?

You will notice in this verse as Saul begins to prophesy among the prophets, the people of Israel ask a very astute question, "Who is Saul's father?" The people of Israel were very familiar with prophets and the operation of prophets. Let us keep in mind, that to understand the prophetic, it was a cultural norm for them. If there is any nation that is going to understand prophets it most certainly is Israel. They not only understood prophetic principles but they also understood the principle of lineage. They wanted to know who gave Saul his personal apolyo. Even though Saul prophesied and Saul had a flow and a gift, the people of Israel still asked the question, "Who is Saul's father?" In other words, who is responsible for his endorsement and who has sent him? There is not one apostle mentioned in Scripture wherein we are unable to trace him back to a chief apostolic father. Even the great apostle Paul found it necessary to go to Jerusalem and submit his ministry to the chief apostles, James and Peter. Paul later comments, "... they added nothing to me." Paul was speaking solely of the content of his gospel message and nothing more. Paul purposed to fulfill all righteousness in that he aligned himself with divine order and structure as he submitted his apostolic ministry to a chief apostolic father.

CHAPTER 9

THE APOSTOLIC SUMMONS

There is another dimension of the apostolic: the apostolic summons. This is a time wherein the apostles are summoned by a chief apostolic father for a specific reason. The Greek word here is the word metapempo.

The word metapempo means to be sent for or to be summoned. This is actually a time when a chief apostolic father will summon his apostolic sons and / or daughters for specific purpose. We see this word used when Peter was summoned to go to the house of Cornelius. Peter was actually summoned by the Angel of the Lord who gave a direct command to Cornelius to summon Peter. Without having to go into a deep theological teaching, let it be clearly understood that the Angel of the Lord was Christ, Himself.

Acts 10:5 (KJV)

5. And now send men to Joppa, and call for one Simon, whose surname is Peter:

The Angel of the Lord is Christ who is Chief Apostle. They note the fact that this was an apostolic summons by a chief apostle. Peter was wise enough to not only detect the authority in the summons, but to also have a proper response. The apostolic summons is a very critical test for many apostolic sons. These sons sometimes come under a "spiritual litmus test," so to speak. It determines if, as an apostolic son, does he or she still recognize the authority over his or her life even though they may be functioning as accomplished apostles.

Numbers 10:4 (KJV)

4. And if they blow but with one trumpet, then the princes, which are heads of the thousands of Israel, shall gather themselves unto thee.

In the Israeli wilderness camp, there were specific times of summons which was prompted by the blowing of trumpets. If you notice carefully, this gathering was only for the princes and heads of the thousands of Israel. These were the Old Testament apostles over the various tribes and clans of Israel. This occurred at specific times when they were summoned by directives from Moses, God's chief apostle in the house of Moses.

Numbers 16:12-14 (KJV)

12. And Moses sent to call Dathan and Abiram, the sons of Eliab: which said, We will not come up:

13. Is it a small thing that thou hast brought us up out of a land that floweth with milk and honey, to kill us in the wilderness, except thou make thyself altogether a prince over us?

14. Moreover thou hast not brought us into a land that floweth with milk and honey, or given us inheritance of fields and vineyards: wilt thou put out the eyes of these men? we will not come up.

In this particular passage of scripture, Moses sends for Dathan and Abiram. The word sent here is the Hebrew word shelah, a word we mentioned in previous chapters. This usage of sent is where we ultimately derive the word apostle. Within this framework, Moses functions in the office of chief apostle, as he summons these apostolic sons to come and stand before him. If you will notice, in this case, Dathan and Abiram responded by saying, "...we will not come up." How sad a response this was because it readily revealed rebellion at work in their hearts. In fully discerning the chief apostolic authority that rested upon the life of Moses it is interesting to note how Moses responded to this act of rebellion. Ultimately, Moses calls Dathan, Abiram and both of their entire families before him. Notice what Moses says in verse 28.

Numbers 16:28 (KJV)

28. And Moses said, Hereby ye shall know that the LORD hath sent me to do all these works; for I have not done them of mine own mind.

Moses references the fact that God sent him to do this work. Again, the word sent is the same Hebrew word we mentioned before, shelah. This is the Old Testament term for apostle. One of the derivatives of the word shelah is the word shelahed which means to be deputized or given authority. You will notice he also said, "...I did not do this of my own mind." He was reasserting the fact that the authority in which he operated was given to him by God. In reading the rest of the story you will see the results of their disobedience. Note: Today, we may not witness these occurrences literally and we understand that, but there are still spiritual ramifications that result from this type of rebellion.

Many apostolic sons have walked away, refused to obey an apostolic summons by their apostolic father, and in fact, they have fallen into a pit along with all that pertains to them. Remember the scripture that says, "... to whom much is given, of him much is required." If your authority increases, correspondingly, your responsibility increases. Remember what the Roman centurion said to Jesus, "...I'm a man of authority and a man under authority."

CHAPTER 10

APOSTOLIC SUPPLY

There is another very important apostolic role called the supplying apostle. This particular apostolic grace, rests on apostles who are called to be suppliers to chief apostles. Albeit, though this is a somewhat hidden role, it does not result in it being any less important. The supplying apostle enables apostles to effectively go forward when they have sons and daughters who clearly recognize their role of being a supplier. The Greek word for this particular type of apostle is the word:

Propempō': The word means to send forth, to accompany, or aid in travel.

Due to the arduous work and difficulty of apostolic ministry, it is very important that there are apostles who function as "supplying apostles". In the Old Testament they were called mighty men of valor. The word valor in the Old Testament is a very interesting word. The word valor speaks to the character of a person as well as to their courage. Interestingly enough, how about the fact that the word also means wealth?

Ḥayil: The word means strength, it means wealth, or it means coverage.

David was accompanied by mighty men of valor. These are men that had both money and supply. These men were able to assist David in the fulfillment of whatever ministerial need that God had given David.

Just as it was yesterday, so it is today. There is a need for the mighty men of valor to step up because they, in fact, are the apostles of supply. These men are set as part of the apostolic team of any apostle to be supplying apostles. They help the work of God go forward by giving out of their finances, their resources and their talents.

Romans 15:24 (KJV)

24. Whensoever I take my journey into Spain, I will come to you: for I trust to see you in my journey, and to be brought on my way thitherward by you, if first I be somewhat filled with your company.

Paul, in his letter to the church in Rome used this phrase, "And to Be Brought on My Way by You." The Greek word here is the Greek word Propempō. In other words, Paul was saying he expected them to supply what he needed to continue on in his apostolic mission. When an apostle does not have a company of people who have discerned the need to be apostolic suppliers to his work, then that particular apostle is hindered and unable to fulfill the apostolic mandate assigned him. Hence, we readily see that the supplying apostle is a very, very critical role in the apostolic strategy of warfare.

Today, God is raising up apostolic men and women whose lives have been transformed, changed and impacted by a chief apostle so much so that they are keenly aware they are anointed and appointed as suppliers. Their chief focus is to assist that particular apostle in fulfilling the mandate upon his or her life.

Titus 3:13 (KJV)

13. Bring Zenas the lawyer and Apollos on their journey diligently, that nothing be wanting unto them.

In this epistle to Titus, Paul gives written instructions concerning the lawyer Zenas and Apollos. The Greek word Propempō is translated "bring". In other words, Paul was saying, in modern day vernacular, "Be sure to purchase the airline ticket, pay for the hotel stay and make sure they have ready cash on hand so that they lack nothing." This is what is called real apostolic supply. The Holy Spirit had a very accurate strategy in mind as it pertains to the doctrine of prosperity to the church. The purpose of the doctrine of prosperity was to create apostolic suppliers who are mighty men and women of valor, who walk in an anointing that allows them to go and get wealth so that apostolic ministry can be supplied. Some of these people stand in a duel role. They have a marketplace apostolic call upon them, as well as possessing a supplying apostolic call, so that the gospel of the kingdom might go forth and current day apostles might be supplied.

1 Corinthians 16:10-11 (KJV)

10. Now if Timotheus come, see that he may be with you without fear: for he worketh the work of the Lord, as I also do.

11. Let no man therefore despise him: but conduct him forth in peace, that he may come unto me: for I look for him with the brethren.

In this particular set of verses we see Paul writes a letter which concerns Timothy. The letter is addressed to the leaders of the church at Corinth. Paul admonishes them to make sure that they see to the care of Timothy. He reminds them of the fact that

Timothy is an apostle likened unto him. If you notice in verse 11 he used the term, "...but conduct him forth in peace." Again, we see the Greek word propempo. This time propempo is translated as conduct. In other words, he wants them to know that they need to supply Timothy. Let's also make note that we see the word peace used here as well.

In the Greek, this word is eirēnē; which means prosperity. In other words, Paul instructs them to send Timothy forward with prosperity. Paul, in no uncertain terms meant don't just give him minimal supply or even sufficient supply, but make sure this is an abundant supply so that when Timothy leaves your presence, he should have more than enough. When he leaves you and you conduct him forth, or propempo him he should have prosperity. Make no mistake about it, this was the purpose and still is the purpose for God's release of the prosperity message into the body of Christ. It was designed to create apostolic suppliers, who would be able to supply apostolic ministries, as well as apostles, in the work that they are called to do.

CHAPTER 11

FROM TEMPORARY TO PERMANENT

For every believer there is a process of divine progression. Progression is a natural part of kingdom development and this development brings an increase. All progression goes through a process; it is the process of progression. God never intended for you to stay where you are without growth and expansion. This is clearly seen in apostolic development. The place of the "temporary pempo apostolic anointing," is still temporary. God desires for apostolic people to at least move out of apprenticeship into full measure. We have to remember, however, it is of critical importance to be willing to move through the necessary steps of this process of progression. We will see this more clearly as we look at the next set of Scriptures. The scriptures will allow us to more fully understand the process of progression from pempo to a permanent apostolic license.

Acts 15:22 (KJV)

22. Then pleased it the apostles and elders, with the whole church, to send chosen men of their own company to Antioch with Paul and Barnabas; namely, Judas surnamed Barsabas, and Silas, chief men among the brethren:

In this particular verse we see the culmination of one of the very first major apostolic conferences; a conference where major decisions were made about the doctrinal status of the primitive apostolic church. Once the elders and chief apostles made their decisions, there was a need for the information to be delivered and disseminated among the other churches. The elders, therefore chose two men, Judas and Silas as 'sent men' who were chosen out of the midst of the apostles. In other words these were men who were a part of an apostolic team but as of yet they were not fully licensed as apostles. They were, however, given a temporary apostolic license or pempo anointing to go forth on a temporary assignment. The Scripture also notes that these men were prophets, as well. It is important to understand, that all apostles are prophets, but all prophets are not apostles. Many who are standing currently in the office of the prophet will from time to time be commissioned with temporary apostolic assignments as preparation for the promotion. It is also important to take note that these men did not go beyond their measure of rule. Measure of rule is very important to understand in regard to the apostle. As we continue to study Scripture, we later see Paul makes reference to Silas as an apostle.

1 Thessalonians 1:1-6 (KJV)

1. Paul, and Silvanus, and Timotheus, unto the church of the Thessalonians which is in God the Father and in the Lord Jesus Christ: Grace be unto you, and peace, from God our Father, and the Lord Jesus Christ.

2. We give thanks to God always for you all, making mention of you in our prayers;

3 Remembering without ceasing your work of faith, and labour of love, and patience of hope in our Lord Jesus Christ, in the sight of God and our Father;

4. Knowing, brethren beloved, your election of God

5. For our gospel came not unto you in word only, but also in power, and in the Holy Ghost, and in much assurance; as ye know what manner of men we were among you for your sake.

6. And ye became followers of us, and of the Lord, having received the word in much affliction, with joy of the Holy Ghost:

Paul greets the church in Thessalonica. In verses five and six Paul says, "...our gospel came not unto you in a word, but also in power." When Paul uses the term, "our gospel," he is in fact saying, "....the gospel that Silas, Timothy and I preached." (Not verbatim). Paul actually acknowledges these men as apostles in their own right. In verse six, Paul says, "....and you became followers of us." Paul does not say followers of Paul or all of the members of the Pauline network of churches, but followers of us collectively. This further embraces Paul's acknowledgment of Timothy and Silas as apostles. These were men that moved forward in the apostolic progression. Timothy and Silas faithfully walked with Paul as temporary apostles and accompanying apostles until they became apostles in their own right.

How can it possibly be that today we have people saved one year and one year later they are apostles? How can this be without ever having gone through any form of apprenticeship? Does God break the rules with them only, yet requires everyone else to go by the rules in order that they may become apostolically licensed? This is absolutely not possible and this is absolutely not so. Many of these people who make these claims are false apostles not having any level of confirming apostolic authority or apostolic grace.

1 Thessalonians 2:1-6 (KJV)

1. For yourselves, brethren, know our entrance in unto you, that it was not in vain:

2. But even after that we had suffered before, and were shamefully entreated, as ye know, at Philippi, we were bold in our God to speak unto you the gospel of God with much contention.

3. For our exhortation was not of deceit, nor of uncleanness, nor in guile:

4. But as we were allowed of God to be put in trust with the gospel, even so we speak; not as pleasing men, but God, which trieth our hearts.

5. For neither at any time used we flattering words, as ye know, nor a cloke of covetousness; God is witness:

6. Nor of men sought we glory, neither of you, nor yet of others, when we might have been burdensome, as the apostles of Christ.

Here again, it is important for us to to reiterate and clearly emphasize how Paul spoke in terms of his apostolic team. When we read Paul's writings that speak of the apostolic team that accompanied him, we frequently see Paul use the term "we" or "our". If you will notice in verse six, Paul is very explicit when he says, "... the apostles of Christ." Paul does not say 'apostle' in a singular sense, but he used the term apostles in the plural form, which clearly denotes Paul's reference of the men that accompany him. Paul had respect of these men as apostles who fully came into their apostleship in their own right. These men had successfully gone through the maturation process, having started out as accompanying apostles with Paul, but ended well because they ultimately stood in apostolic offices of their own.

This is the divine process of progression, the necessary requirements of true apostolic growth and development. If this model is ever abandoned, we will be inundated with unseasoned novices who will trespass over into God's kingdom, touting "bogus apostolic calls" and walking in "bogus apostolic offices," as well as making claims that are not verifiable.

I have personally witnessed many who lay claim to an apostolic call because they have gone through some apostolic ordination mill with someone who has conducted some kind of apostolic ordination service. Once the so-called ordination service is concluded, these people go forth in claim to be apostles; with full reliance on their organizational skill set as a springboard to bring together a network of churches under specific civil structure. These people proceed forward in reference to themselves as apostles, but there are no supernatural signs operating in their lives. In many cases, they don't even possess a simple gift of prophecy. Every one of these infractions are violations and transgressions which shifts them into the area of trespass and presumption.

In closing, I will submit that there are those who have committed these trespasses out of ignorance, simply because the apostolic restoration is still new and not fully understood in the body of Christ today. With that said, please understand that this in no way excuses those, however, who have committed these infractions, with a full understanding of exactly what they were doing and proceeded to do it, anyway and out of shear arrogance. It is implicit in this season of apostolic restoration that we have the divine order and the divine structure that God always required under the Old Covenant. He requires no less under the New. Divine order and divine structure is all God moves within and this must be in place if we want His fire and His rain to fall.

1 Corinthians 14:39 (KJV)

"...Let all things be done decent and in order."

49

Notes

Notes

Book Onderring Information

Other Books Written By: Chief Apostle Joseph L. Prude

Prophetic Laboratory

Office of the Dream Master

Dream Masters College Curriculum

Female Apostle

The False Bishop

Restoring Healing in The African American Church

The Creation

Ministry of the Apostle

Office of the Chief Apostle

Ministry of the Prophet

Ministry of the Prophet Level 2

The Certified Prophetic Trainer

The Highjacking of the Gospel

The Secrets of His Presence

The Mystery of Angels

The False Teaching of the Tallit

How to Interpret Any Dream

APOSTOLIC METRONS

Interracial Marriage

Prophetic Proverbs

The Ministry of Fasting and Prayer

josephprude@gmail.com

Order books on amazon.com

or

www.ajpministries.com

ISBN 978-1-5136-1835-7